‖‖‖ ‖‖ ‖‖‖ ‖‖ ‖ ‖‖‖‖‖ ‖‖ ‖‖‖‖ ‖‖ ‖‖‖ ‖ ‖‖‖ ‖ ‖‖‖

◁ W9-BGP-669

DATE DUE		
1-29-98	JA 28 '05	
2·25·98		
3.17.98	NO 09'05	·
4-9-98		
-28-98	OCT 1 9 2006	
6·1·98		
MR 31 '00	DEC 1 1 2007	
SE 28 '00	DEC 1 9 2007	
MR 8'02	OCT 1 5 2009	
OC 21 03		
OC 13'04		

92
BET

Majewski, Stephen.

Sports great Jerome Bettis

MIDDLE SCHOOL PLAINVILLE LIC
PLAINVILLE CONNECTICUT 06062

652805 01723   00026B   002

SPORTS GREAT JEROME BETTIS

—Sports Great Books—

BASEBALL

Sports Great Jim Abbott
0-89490-395-0/ Savage

Sports Great Barry Bonds
0-89490-595-3/ Sullivan

Sports Great Bobby Bonilla
0-89490-417-5/ Knapp

Sports Great Roger Clemens
0-89490-284-9/ Devaney

Sports Great Orel Hershiser
0-89490-389-6/ Knapp

Sports Great Bo Jackson
0-89490-281-4/ Knapp

Sports Great Greg Maddux
0-89490-873-1/ Thornley

Sports Great Kirby Puckett
0-89490-392-6/ Aaseng

Sports Great Cal Ripken, Jr.
0-89490-387-X/ Macnow

Sports Great Nolan Ryan
0-89490-394-2/ Lace

Sports Great Darryl Strawberry
0-89490-291-1/ Torres & Sullivan

BASKETBALL

Sports Great Charles Barkley
0-89490-386-1/ Macnow

Sports Great Larry Bird
0-89490-368-3/ Kavanagh

Sports Great Muggsy Bogues
0-89490-876-6/ Rekela

Sports Great Patrick Ewing
0-89490-369-1/ Kavanagh

Sports Great Anfernee Hardaway
0-89490-758-1/ Rekela

**Sports Great Magic Johnson
(Revised and Expanded)**
0-89490-348-9/ Haskins

Sports Great Michael Jordan
0-89490-370-5/ Aaseng

Sports Great Karl Malone
0-89490-599-6/ Savage

Sports Great Reggie Miller
0-89490-874-X/ Thornley

Sports Great Alonzo Mourning
0-89490-875-8/ Fortunato

Sports Great Hakeem Olajuwon
0-89490-372-1/ Knapp

Sports Great Shaquille O'Neal
0-89490-594-5/ Sullivan

Sports Great Scottie Pippen
0-89490-755-7/ Bjarkman

Sports Great David Robinson
0-89490-373-X/ Aaseng

Sports Great Dennis Rodman
0-89490-759-X/ Thornley

Sports Great John Stockton
0-89490-598-8/ Aaseng

Sports Great Isiah Thomas
0-89490-374-8/ Knapp

Sports Great Dominique Wilkins
0-89490-754-9/ Bjarkman

FOOTBALL

Sports Great Troy Aikman
0-89490-593-7/ Macnow

Sports Great Jerome Bettis
0-89490-872-3/Majewski

Sports Great John Elway
0-89490-282-2/ Fox

Sports Great Jim Kelly
0-89490-670-4/ Harrington

Sports Great Joe Montana
0-89490-371-3/ Kavanagh

Sports Great Jerry Rice
0-89490-419-1/ Dickey

Sports Great Barry Sanders
0-89490-418-3/ Knapp

Sports Great Herschel Walker
0-89490-207-5/ Benagh

HOCKEY

Sports Great Wayne Gretzky
0-89490-757-3/ Rappoport

Sports Great Mario Lemieux
0-89490-596-1/ Knapp

TENNIS

Sports Great Steffi Graf
0-89490-597-X/ Knapp

Sports Great Pete Sampras
0-89490-756-5/ Sherrow

SPORTS GREAT JEROME BETTIS

Stephen Majewski

—Sports Great Books—

Enslow Publishers, Inc.

44 Fadem Road	PO Box 38
Box 699	Aldershot
Springfield, NJ 07081	Hants GU12 6BP
USA	UK

Copyright © 1997 by Stephen Majewski

All rights reserved.

No part of this book may be reproduced by any means
without the written permission of the publisher.

Library of Congress Cataloging-in-Publication Data

Majewski, Stephen.
    Sports great Jerome Bettis / Stephen Majewski.
       p. cm. — (Sports great books)
    Includes index.
    Summary: Profiles the life and career of Jerome Bettis, superstar linebacker for the
St. Louis Rams.
    ISBN 0-89490-872-3
    1. Bettis, Jerome—Juvenile literature. 2. Football players—United States—
Biography—Juvenile literature. [1. Bettis, Jerome. 2. Football players.
3. Afro-Americans—Biography.] I. Title II. Series
GV939.B48M35   1997
796.332'092—dc20
[B]   96-25400
                                                     CIP
                                                        AC

Printed in the United States of America.

10 9 8 7 6 5 4 3 2 1

Photo Credits: Courtesy of the Los Angeles Rams, pp. 9, 11, 34; Courtesy of the
St. Louis Rams, pp. 17, 36, 40, 45, 47, 49, 53, 55, 58; University of Notre Dame
Sports Information Department, pp. 20, 26, 29.

Cover Photo: Mike Fabus, Pittsburgh Steelers.

Contents

Acknowledgments 6

Chapter 1 7

Chapter 2 15

Chapter 3 23

Chapter 4 33

Chapter 5 43

Chapter 6 51

Career Statistics 60

Where to Write 61

Index 63

Acknowledgments

I am grateful to Marci Moran and Sandy Schenck of the St. Louis Rams Public Relations Department and to John Heisler, sports information director at the University of Notre Dame, for their help in providing photographs. Thanks also to Dave Gross, Mark Passarella, and Lamont Smith. Special thanks to Libby Majewski for her editorial assistance.

Chapter 1

The year was 1993. The Los Angeles Rams had a dismal 3-9 record. They were visiting the highly favored New Orleans Saints, who came into the game with a 7-5 record. One of the few bright spots in the Rams' frustrating 1993 season was their 245-pound rookie running back, Jerome Bettis. In just his first season in the National Football League (NFL), Bettis was running neck and neck with Emmitt Smith of the Dallas Cowboys for the league rushing title.

The Saints were one of the NFL's better teams at stopping the run. They had defeated the Rams seven straight times. Bettis would have to put forth an extra effort to give the Rams a chance to beat the Saints. He was also battling to keep himself in the race for the NFL rushing title. Just two minutes and five seconds into the game, however, disaster struck Jerome Bettis and the Rams.

On first and ten from his own 30-yard line, Jerome ran into a stack of Saints' defenders. While trying to drive forward for additional yardage, Saints' linebacker James Williams stripped the football from Bettis's hands. Another Saints' linebacker, Sam Mills, picked up the ball and raced into the end zone for a touchdown. The Saints led the Rams 7-0.

The New Orleans home crowd let loose a deafening roar of appreciation, but Bettis kept his cool. He was angry with himself but promised to get even. "Somebody was going to have to pay for that," Bettis said.

Following a 10-yard run by Bettis, the Rams managed to kick a field goal and cut the Saints' lead to 7-3. On the Rams' next possession, Bettis made the Saints pay for their earlier touchdown. From his own 29-yard line, Rams quarterback T. J. Rubley pitched the football to Bettis. Offensive guard Leo Goeas and fullback Tim Lester made a huge hole on the right side of the line of scrimmage. Jerome Bettis darted through the hole, shook off a Saints tackler, and raced all the way to the end zone for a touchdown. The 71-yard touchdown run put the Rams ahead 10-7.

Every running back's goal is to rush for at least 125 yards in a game. After just one quarter Jerome Bettis already had 125 yards on twelve carries. A bruised abdomen, however, made it difficult for Bettis to breathe. The injury forced him to sit out the second quarter. The Rams were unable to score without Jerome Bettis in the game, while the Saints kicked two field goals. At halftime, the Saints held a 13-10 lead. If the Rams were going to win the game, they needed Jerome Bettis to play in the second half, which he did despite his injury.

To start the third quarter, the Rams' special teams took its turn to score. The Saints' kick returner fumbled the second-half kick off. Rams safety Deral Boykin picked up the ball at the 6-yard line and took it into the end zone to give the Rams a 17-13 lead.

The Saints were geared to stop Jerome Bettis in the second half, but the Rams kept giving him the ball anyway. Leading 17-13, the Rams marched 80 yards in 13 plays for a

Jerome Bettis finds a hole in the defense. In his rookie year Bettis had a
71-yard touchdown run against New Orleans.

touchdown. Jerome Bettis ran the football on 10 of the 13 plays for 51 yards. Behind Bettis, the Rams made it all the way to the 11-yard line.

On the Rams thirteenth play of the drive, it seemed certain that Jerome Bettis would get the ball again. Instead, quarterback T. J. Rubley faked a handoff to Bettis to draw the Saints' defenders away from the Rams' receivers. Tight end Pat Carter got open in the end zone and Rubley threw the ball to him for a touchdown. Although the Saints blocked the extra point kick, the Rams increased their lead to 23-13. The Saints managed to score a touchdown in the fourth quarter, but the Rams hung on to win, 23-20.

Jerome Bettis finished the game with 212 yards rushing on 28 carries, an average of 7.6 yards per carry. It was one of the best rookie-rushing performances in NFL history. Bettis was just the eighth rookie to rush for more than 200 yards in a single game, and his 212 yards was the fourth highest total for a rookie. No NFL rookie had rushed for 200 yards in a single game since Bo Jackson did it in 1987.

Near the end of the game, Bettis let the Saints know that his rushing performance was not a fluke. On a run for 22 yards, Bettis had his helmet ripped from his head as he was tackled near the Saints' sideline. Jerome Bettis got up and looked at the Saints' players. "I just wanted to show them, 'Hey, I'm for real. Here I am. Get used to me.'"

Jerome Bettis was the first Rams rookie to rush for more than 200 yards in a game since Tom Wilson did it in 1956. His 212 yards was the sixth highest single-game total in Rams history. Bettis's stats were impressive considering that he played only three-quarters of the game. The Rams were also without their two best offensive linemen, tackle Jackie Slater and guard Tom Newberry, who were injured.

Jerome Bettis's 212 yards rushing against the New Orleans

Bettis once ran for 212 yards against the New Orleans Saints. This was the fourth-highest single-game rushing total for a rookie player.

Saints also pushed him over the 1,000-yard mark for the season. Like rushing for 125 yards in a game, every running back also wants to rush for more than 1,000 yards in a season. Jerome Bettis became the first Rams rookie running back to rush for more than 1,000 yards in a season since Eric Dickerson did it in 1983. For his efforts, Bettis was named the National Football Conference (NFC) offensive player of the week.

Jerome Bettis remained modest after his outstanding game. "We just wanted to run the football," he said. "We wanted to really pound it. I didn't think we'd be that successful though. It's a great feeling. I never got 1,000 yards at Notre Dame [where Bettis played college football]."

Rams head coach Chuck Knox had high praise for Jerome Bettis after the game. "Bettis is outstanding. I mean the guy has been that from day one."

Even the Saints were impressed with Bettis. "It was amazing," Saints linebacker Sam Mills said after the game. "I don't expect anyone to do that. I don't expect a Hall of Famer to come out and play like that against our defense."

A unique blend of power and speed enabled Jerome Bettis to perform so well during his rookie season. Coach Knox knew Bettis had the athletic ability to be a great running back. "It's amazing that a guy that big, that is 240 pounds, has the nimbleness, quick feet, and the great balance that he has," says Coach Knox. "He's as good as any back I've ever coached."

Coach Knox also noticed how well his rookie running back responded to adversity, such as fumbling early in the game against the Saints. "That game showed [Bettis] has a lot of resiliency," said Coach Knox. "That he can overcome something bad that happened to him and look at it as a temporary setback. He didn't become discouraged. He kept wanting the ball, and we gave it to him."

Because the NFL has 280- to 300-pound defensive

linemen who are fast, Jerome Bettis made a conscious effort to run aggressively when he entered the NFL. This impressed Coach Knox. "The great thing about him is that he breaks so many tackles. We [the coaches] judge backs by how many yards they get after the first contact. Jerome gets yardage not only after the first contact, but second and third contact. He just keeps on going," said Coach Knox. Jerome Bettis's bruising running style earned him the nickname "Battering Ram."

Teams scheduled to play the Rams know that they have to make special preparations for Jerome Bettis. "He's a big back, and if you don't come at him with everything, he'll hurt you," said former New York Giants linebacker Carlton Bailey. Playing football on the streets of Detroit as a child is where Jerome Bettis learned to punish defenders.

Chapter 2

Jerome Bettis made the Pro Bowl his first two seasons in the NFL. That is quite an accomplishment for someone like Bettis who did not start playing organized football until he was a freshman in high school. While growing up in Detroit, Michigan, he did not even dream of playing professional football. Jerome Bettis had other ideas for his future. He wanted to be a professional bowler. "I didn't have the typical fantasy of wanting to be a pro football player since I was six years old. That wasn't my life," said Bettis. "I wanted to be a pro bowler, and I still do."

When he was seven years old, Jerome's mother, Gladys, kindled his interest in bowling. "My mom started us bowling as a way to get us off the streets and get us doing something productive on a daily basis," explained Jerome. "It was a good outlet. Bowling kept us busy on the weekends and schoolwork kept us busy during the week." Jerome's mother also pushed bowling because it was safer than sports requiring physical contact. The last thing she wanted to see was her children getting hurt playing a rough sport. Jerome,

his older brother, Johnnie, his older sister, Kimberly, and his parents took bowling very seriously. At one time or another all three children have each been the family champion.

Jerome excelled at bowling. He won the state bowling championship and competed in tournaments around the country. His idol was Earl Anthony, a successful professional bowler. "Earl Anthony was my man," says Jerome. "I had an Earl Anthony Magnum 6 ball." Jerome simply loved to bowl and did not even think about playing football.

The competition in bowling has helped Bettis in his football career. "Bowling has been a challenge for me," says Bettis. "It's really helped me to compete within myself because if I was going to be a good bowler, I had to make myself a good bowler. I carried that over in that regard to say, 'Hey! If I'm going to be a quality football player, I have to make myself be a quality football player.'"

Eventually, Jerome displayed his athletic ability in areas other than bowling. Jerome liked to do whatever Johnnie did, including playing football on the streets of Detroit. It was there that Jerome developed his punishing running style. Jerome was four years younger than his brother and was one of the smaller kids in the neighborhood. Johnnie's friends often purposely hit Jerome on the head after they had tackled him. After a few headaches, Jerome realized that he had to stand up for himself if he was going to play football with the bigger kids. "I made it a point to hit those guys back," Jerome recalled. "I told myself, 'Next time I get the ball, I'm going to find them, and when I find them I'm going to give them a forearm or something.' That's how I picked up always wanting to hit somebody." One day Jerome's uncle, a high school football coach in Detroit, saw him playing football in the street with his friends. He said to Jerome's mother, "The boy's got talent."

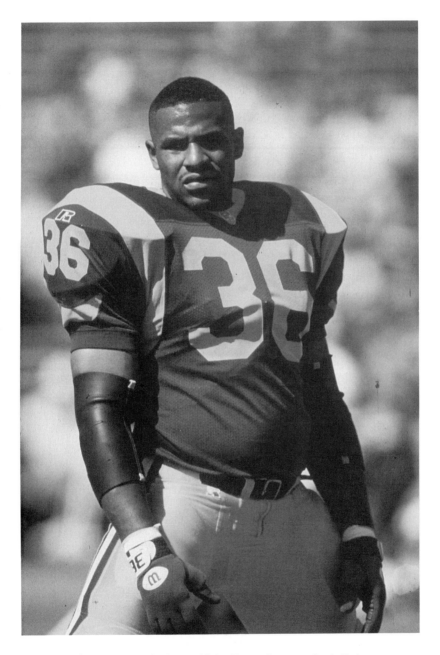

As a child Jerome Bettis did not think of becoming a pro football player. After making the All-Pro team in each of his first two NFL seasons, however, it is safe to say that he made the right choice.

Jerome remained devoted to bowling, but football quickly became an important part of his life. He realized that his athletic ability could help him attend college. If Jerome played football well in high school, universities might be willing to pay for his tuition if he played for them. "At the time, I was looking at the bigger picture. I felt that my father wouldn't be able to support the family and send my brother and sister and me to school," said Bettis. "So, I wanted to find a way that I could send myself to school. I saw sports as that outlet." Jerome had good reasons for choosing football over other sports. "I figured I was a little too short for basketball, and I wouldn't catch that shot down the third-base line, so I said, 'Hey, I've got to play football,'" recalled Bettis.

During his freshman year of high school, Jerome lived with his aunt on the other side of town so that he could play football at Henry Ford High School. There Jerome began to dream of playing in the NFL. Jerome's mother was nervous at the thought of her son playing a contact sport, but she did not stop him from playing football. She went to every game and brought him home on weekends. Watching Jerome play eased any lingering fear for her son's safety. "I had to be there to make sure everything was OK," said Jerome's mother. ". . . so I had to see myself how he played. That's when I started to enjoy him playing the game."

After his freshman year, Jerome transferred to David MacKenzie High School to play football closer to home. There he had an outstanding high school career. Jerome made the varsity team all three years at MacKenzie and was a team captain his junior and senior years. On offense he played running back and on defense he played middle linebacker. Jerome earned All-State honors for both positions and was a high school All-American linebacker.

As a senior, Jerome carried the ball 123 times for 1,355

yards and scored 14 touchdowns. From his middle linebacker position on defense, he recorded a total of 157 tackles for the season, averaging 15 tackles per game. MacKenzie won the West Division title of the Detroit Public School League, and Jerome was named Michigan's football player of the year.

Experts considered Jerome Bettis one of the top one hundred high school football players in America, and recruiters from all over the country wanted him to play football for their university. Although Jerome could have attended almost any university, he had to make the difficult decision of which one would be best for him. He narrowed his choices to the University of Michigan and the University of Notre Dame, both national football powers. Michigan wanted Jerome to play linebacker and Notre Dame wanted him to play fullback. At five feet eleven inches, Jerome thought he would have a better chance to make the NFL as a fullback. So he chose to play college football at Notre Dame.

"I looked at my chances and decided I wanted to play fullback. Notre Dame was the one school that was going to give me the best opportunity to play that position," explained Jerome. "Coach [Lou] Holtz promised me coming in that I would be the only fullback he'd recruit for two years. He held true to that."

Some people criticized Jerome Bettis for leaving the state of Michigan to attend Notre Dame. It is located in Indiana. "I got a lot of pressure for leaving the state. It was a decision I made feeling it was best for me," said Bettis. "I felt that at Michigan, ultimately, they'd move me to linebacker because they don't utilize the fullback that much. I think my future would've been in question."

Skip Holtz, a Notre Dame assistant coach and son of Head Coach Lou Holtz, thought Jerome would make a perfect fullback. "He has all the strengths of a good fullback, but he

Jerome Bettis was a fullback for the Notre Dame Fighting Irish.

can also make these incredible cuts and change directions at a split second and then the speed. He has tailback speed. Plus, he likes to hit people, which comes from his days as a linebacker."

Before Jerome decided to play for the Notre Dame Fighting Irish, however, Coach Lou Holtz had to make him another promise. "The biggest problem with Jerome was, he didn't like the fact we wore black shoes and didn't put tape on them," explains Coach Holtz. "After thinking about it, I told Jerome if he came to Notre Dame, I'd let him tape his shoes. He came, taped his shoes, and everybody else wanted to do the same thing. I told them, 'Nope, only Jerome can tape his shoes.'"

Jerome had made his decision. He was going to Notre Dame to play fullback. All he had to do was work his way into the lineup of one of America's best college football teams, not necessarily an easy task.

Chapter 3

Jerome Bettis arrived at the University of Notre Dame as one of the top high school football players in the nation. Notre Dame, however, was full of the best college players in the country. Therefore, Bettis had to make the most of any chance he had to play.

During his freshman year Jerome Bettis played sparingly, but he made the most of his chances. Backing up starting fullback Rodney Culver, Bettis carried the ball 15 times and averaged 7.7 yards per carry for the year. Head Coach Lou Holtz saw so much potential that he made Bettis the starting fullback before his sophomore season and moved Rodney Culver to tailback. "We saw something in [Bettis] as a freshman that led us to believe he would be an excellent fullback," said Coach Holtz. "He's a natural there. He loves the game. He doesn't care whether he blocks or whether he carries the football."

Making Jerome Bettis the starting fullback was a wise move. He went on to have one of the finest seasons in Notre Dame history. In his first start of the 1991 season, Bettis carried the ball 11 times for 111 yards as Notre Dame defeated Indiana, 49-27. Two weeks later, Jerome Bettis racked up 93 yards on 16 carries as the Notre Dame Fighting Irish rolled to a 49-10 victory over the Michigan State Spartans.

Against Stanford, Jerome Bettis had the best day of his career at Notre Dame. He carried the ball 24 times, rushed for 179 yards, and had 3 touchdowns. He also caught a 13-yard touchdown pass from quarterback Rick Mirer. Bettis was the first Notre Dame player to score four times in a game since Anthony Johnson did it against Navy in 1987. *College & Pro Football Newsweekly* named Jerome Bettis its offensive player of the week.

Playing against the Pittsburgh Panthers the following week, Bettis continued to run well. He rumbled for 125 yards on 17 carries and scored 2 touchdowns, including one on a 40-yard run up the middle. Notre Dame routed the Panthers, 42-7, and stayed in the hunt for a national championship.

With his combination of speed and power, Jerome Bettis was redefining the fullback position. Many teams use the fullback primarily to block for the tailback. However, Bettis had the ability to block and run the football. Notre Dame could even use Jerome Bettis as a diversion to open up its offense. With defenses geared to stop Bettis, the quarterback could fake a handoff to him and either throw the ball to a receiver or handoff to a tailback.

"Jerome gives us a real solid threat from tackle to tackle," said Tom Beck, running backs coach for Notre Dame during Jerome's sophomore season. "He's the person who makes the linebackers respect any movement he makes through the line and that opens up play-action fakes, options, and counters going opposite his flow."

Jerome Bettis loved his role as a fullback. "Inflicting pain is the most important thing as a fullback. The only way I can be effective is if I pound it in there. I need to be able to hit somebody. It fuels me. It gets my adrenaline pumping."

After Bettis rushed for 178 yards on 24 carries in Notre Dame's 24-20 victory over the University of Southern California, USC head coach Larry Smith said, "I have yet to see a better college fullback in all my years of coaching college football and I've seen some pretty good ones. Bettis is the best I've ever seen. He is a great football player." To go along with his 178 yards rushing, Jerome Bettis scored 2 touchdowns, one of which came on a 53-yard run, the longest of his college career.

As Bettis neared the end of his sophomore season, he was on target to break Notre Dame's single-season record for touchdowns (18) and rushing yards for a fullback (977). Had he been a junior or senior, and thus better known across the country, Bettis would have been a sure pick for the All-America team. Bill Walsh, who won three Super Bowls as head coach of the San Francisco 49ers, said that Jerome Bettis was the best fullback he had seen in years, college and pro.

Bettis was happy that he chose to play fullback in college rather than linebacker. "So many of the recruiters couldn't understand why I wanted to play fullback. They couldn't understand why anyone would actually want to play fullback when he could play linebacker. That's because so many of those schools looked at the fullback position as just another blocker lined up in the backfield. But I knew I could be more."

While Jerome Bettis was having an outstanding sophomore season, Notre Dame was still hoping to win the national championship. The fifth-ranked Fighting Irish were 8-1 going into their game against the fourteenth-ranked Tennessee Volunteers. Although Bettis rushed for 64 yards on 16 carries and scored one touchdown, Notre Dame suffered a

Unfortunately for Bettis, Notre Dame's loss to Tennessee during his sophomore season ended any hopes of a national title for Notre Dame.

disappointing 35-34 loss. Notre Dame's second loss of the season ended any hopes for a national championship.

Notre Dame ended the regular season at 9-3. Jerome Bettis and quarterback Rick Mirer shared the Notre Dame most valuable player award, as voted by their teammates. Bettis finished the regular season with 972 yards rushing, just five yards short of the Notre Dame single-season record for rushing yards by a fullback. He set Notre Dame single-season records for touchdowns (20) and points (120), finishing fourth nationally in scoring. He was a second-team All-America selection by *Football News* and *College & Pro Football Newsweekly*. All that remained in the season was Notre Dame's final game against the Florida Gators in the Sugar Bowl.

The Fighting Irish were ranked eighteenth in the country going into the game against the third-ranked Gators. With Notre Dame out of the national championship picture, the Fighting Irish simply wanted to play well and build momentum for next year. Playing in front of a national television audience, Jerome Bettis had a tremendous game and led Notre Dame to a 39-28 come-from-behind victory.

With 150 yards and 3 touchdowns on 16 carries, Jerome Bettis won the Miller-Digby Memorial Award as the Sugar Bowl's most valuable player. All of his touchdowns came in the fourth quarter. With Notre Dame trailing 22-17 and just 4:48 remaining in the game, Bettis scored on runs of three, forty-nine, and thirty-nine yards.

During his junior season, Jerome Bettis was a *Football Digest* pre-season All-America pick. He was also a candidate for the Heisman Trophy, an award given to the nation's best college player. *The Sporting News* called Jerome Bettis the best player in college football, regardless of position. With Rick Mirer, another Heisman candidate, at quarterback and

Jerome Bettis at fullback, Notre Dame again had hopes of winning the national championship. In 1991 the Fighting Irish averaged 35.5 points per game, and there was every reason to believe they would average that many in 1992.

Jerome Bettis got off to a blazing start for the Heisman Trophy and the national championship. He rushed for 130 yards and one touchdown on 19 carries as Notre Dame whipped Northwestern, 42-7. After the game Coach Holtz talked about Bettis's performance. "Jerome is just Jerome. He's the man."

Notre Dame's hopes for a national championship suffered a slight setback the next week when the Fighting Irish tied the Michigan Wolverines, 17-17. Jerome Bettis carried the ball 15 times for 82 yards and one touchdown. Coach Holtz received a lot of criticism for running the ball on first and second down with the score tied and less than a minute remaining in the game. Bettis, however, refused to criticize his coach. "I was not surprised at the [play] calls. If he felt a run would go, we should have executed well enough so the run would go. If he called two running plays, there was a reason for it."

After the disappointing tie with Michigan, Notre Dame beat Michigan State, 52-31. Jerome Bettis ran for 76 yards on 14 carries. With Bettis running the ball well, the Fighting Irish continued their quest for the national championship. In a 48-0 blowout against Purdue, he rushed the ball 18 times for 93 yards and 2 touchdowns, including one that went for twenty-four yards.

After two easy victories, Notre Dame's next game of the season came against Stanford. Bill Walsh, the coach who guided the San Francisco 49ers to three Super Bowl victories, had returned to college ranks as the head coach of Stanford. If the Fighting Irish hoped to win the national championship,

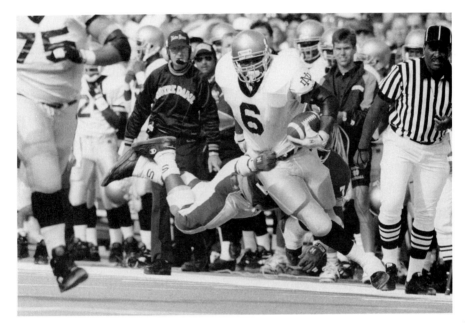

Although Bettis played only three seasons at Notre Dame, he is one of the greatest fullbacks in the school's history.

they could not afford to lose this game. Everyone expected a close contest.

Notre Dame jumped out to a 16-0 lead. But the game slipped away and Stanford came back to win, 33-16. Both quarterback Rick Mirer and Jerome Bettis, two Heisman Trophy candidates, had a difficult day. Mirer connected on only 13 of 38 passes. Bettis ran for just 54 yards, and, to make matters worse, he fumbled twice. Bettis actually had more yards receiving (56) than rushing. With Notre Dame's record at 3-1-1, their national championship dreams fizzled.

"When Coach came over to me after the first fumble, he said, 'Stay positive,'" recalled Bettis. "Whenever you lose a turnover battle like that you can't expect to win the football game."

Like all great players, Jerome Bettis held his head high after the tough loss to Stanford and came back strong for the next game. He ran for 94 yards and 3 touchdowns on just 13 carries, as Notre Dame crushed Pittsburgh, 52-21. For his efforts, Bettis was named the ESPN/VISA player of the game. One week later, he rushed the ball 21 times for 113 yards and 2 touchdowns.

Against Penn State, Bettis showed that he could be a valuable receiver as well as runner. The Fighting Irish trailed the Nittany Lions 16-9 with just twenty-five seconds remaining in the game. On fourth down, quarterback Rick Mirer looked off tight end Irv Smith. Mirer looped the ball over the middle to Bettis for a 3-yard touchdown. This brought the Fighting Irish within one point of the Nittany Lions. "Rick and I have run that play so many times, it's like second nature to us," said Bettis. A two-point conversion gave Notre Dame a dramatic 17-16 victory.

To close out the regular season, Jerome Bettis rushed for 89 yards and one touchdown in a 31-23 win over USC.

Despite being slowed by an ankle injury during the second half of the season, Bettis managed to rush the ball for 825 yards. *Football News* made him an honorable mention All-America pick. Notre Dame finished the regular season with an impressive 9-1-1 record. They earned the right to play the 12-0 Texas A&M Aggies in the Cotton Bowl.

The Aggies hoped to go undefeated, but Notre Dame defeated Texas A&M, 28-3, with a stingy defense and a dynamic offense. Bettis played extremely well in the Cotton Bowl, rushing the ball for 75 yards. He ran for 2 touchdowns and caught a 26-yard touchdown pass. It was his second straight three-touchdown performance in a bowl game.

After outstanding sophomore and junior seasons, many experts thought Bettis would enter the NFL draft. Bettis, however, had a difficult time deciding whether to stay in college or leave to enter the NFL. "You have such a big game and you're on such an emotional high right now, you think you can do anything," he said after the Cotton Bowl. "You have to come back down to reality and really think about what you want to do." If he entered the NFL he could help his family financially. With his father working two jobs, this was a prime consideration. If he stayed in school, he would again be a contender for the Heisman Trophy. It was not an easy decision.

Finally, he decided to leave Notre Dame and pursue his dream of playing professional football. After such an outstanding college career, football analysts expected Bettis to be a first-round pick in the NFL draft. His performance in the Cotton Bowl influenced his decision to enter the draft. "It told me I am ready to go," said Jerome. "I feel I need to go on to the next level."

Jerome Bettis left Notre Dame as one of the greatest fullbacks in the school's history. He ranked fourteenth in career rushing yards with 1,912 yards, sixth in career rushing touchdowns with 27, and fifth in overall touchdowns (rushing and receiving) with 33. For his career, Bettis averaged 5.7 yards per rush. Reflecting on his college career, he said it had been a "great experience for me, but now it's time to move on in my career."

Chapter 4

The Los Angeles Rams made Jerome Bettis the tenth selection in the 1993 NFL draft. The Rams had not won more than six games since 1989, when they won a total of eleven games. On the bright side, the Rams considered Jerome Bettis a key ingredient in their effort to build a winning team.

Although the Rams were not a strong team, their head coach was Chuck Knox. Coach Knox was in his twenty-first year as an NFL head coach. Nicknamed "Ground Chuck" for his fondness of the running game, Knox had a reputation for turning losing teams into winners and, important for Jerome Bettis, developing good running backs.

In college Jerome Bettis played fullback, but he would play tailback for the Rams. Coach Knox brought his rookie along slowly. To begin the season, Bettis backed up veteran running back Cleveland Gary. He carried the ball 5 times for 24 yards in the Rams' season-opening 36-6 loss to the Packers.

In the Rams' second game, Bettis gave the coaches a glimpse of his potential. Cleveland Gary started the game but was forced to leave with a thigh bruise. Bettis entered the

The Los Angeles Rams made Jerome Bettis the tenth player selected in the 1993 draft.

game and ran the ball 16 times for 76 yards, including a 29-yard run for his first NFL touchdown. The Rams defeated the Pittsburgh Steelers, 27-0, and improved their record to 1-1.

With Cleveland Gary still injured, Coach Knox gave Jerome Bettis the starting nod against the New York Giants. The Rams were behind almost the entire game. This made it difficult to establish an effective running game. Bettis carried the ball just 13 times for 33 yards as the Giants beat the Rams, 20-10. Against the Houston Oilers, Cleveland Gary returned to the starting lineup and Bettis saw limited action.

As the Rams starting tailback, Cleveland Gary was averaging just 2 yards per carry. Gary started against the New Orleans Saints. But Coach Knox decided it was time to make a change. Gary would now play mostly in passing situations. Bettis would get most of the carries in running situations. It was a wise decision by Coach Knox.

Jerome Bettis carried the ball 22 times for 102 yards against a strong Saints defense. Behind his running, the Rams were in a position to upset the Saints. The Rams trailed the Saints by only a touchdown with five minutes remaining in the third quarter. New Orleans, however, scored 24 unanswered points in the fourth quarter to win, 37-6.

After such a fine running performance, Bettis replaced Cleveland Gary as the Rams starting tailback. No one else started at tailback for the Rams' until the ninth game of the 1995 season when a foot injury sidelined Bettis. Against the Atlanta Falcons, he continued to run well. He rushed for 85 yards and one touchdown on 19 carries. He also caught the football three times for 53 yards. Unfortunately, the Rams lost, 30-24.

The Rams record stood at 2-4. Part of the reason for this was the play of struggling quarterback Jim Everett. In hopes of jump-starting his team, Coach Knox put in T. J. Rubley at

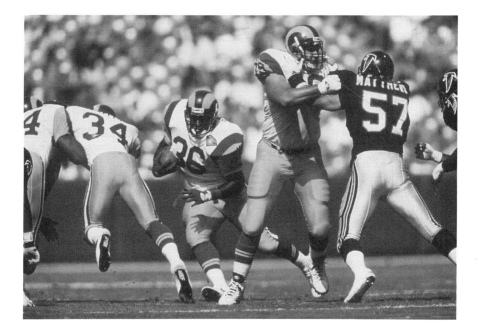

Jerome Bettis replaced Cleveland Gary as the Rams' starting tailback after the fifth game of the 1993 season.

quarterback during a game against the Detroit Lions. Jerome Bettis, quickly becoming a leader on the Rams, talked to both Rubley and Everett about the change. "I told both of them to stay in the game," said Bettis, who rushed for 113 yards on 23 carries. "I told T. J. to settle down and that I would be there for him. And I told Jim to settle down and be ready if his call comes again." Rubley almost pulled out a victory, but the Lions managed to hang on and win, 16-13.

Being a team player, Jerome Bettis felt bad for all the blame Jim Everett was taking for the Rams' 2-5 record. "The fans are being a little too hard on him. He's kind of like the scapegoat for the offense. All the blame is put on him. But that's not fair."

After falling to a 2-7 record, the Rams finally managed a 10-6 win over the Washington Redskins. Jerome Bettis ran the ball for 86 yards on 16 carries. He was thankful for the win. "We really need this to put some fire back into us."

The Rams lost their next two games, but the Battering Ram continued to play like a seasoned veteran. Bettis ran for 133 yards against the San Francisco 49ers and 115 yards against the Phoenix Cardinals. He set the stage for his 212-yard rushing performance against the New Orleans Saints.

With three games remaining in his rookie season, Bettis had already broken the 1,000-yard barrier. "I really thought I was going to play fullback in the NFL. Then to change positions [to tailback] and go for a thousand yards in my first year is just a dream come true," Bettis said.

Jerome Bettis had run himself right into contention for the NFL's rookie of the year award. The Rams had thrown only 28 passes in their last two games. This showed how well Bettis was running the ball. Ironically, Rick Mirer, quarterback for the Seattle Seahawks, was also a candidate for rookie of the year. Bettis and Mirer had competed for the

Heisman Trophy at Notre Dame. Now they were competing for rookie of the year honors in the NFL.

Asked about the most surprising rookies of 1993, Bettis made a point to compliment Mirer. "I think Rick has been the biggest surprise. It's harder being a quarterback. You've got to learn the offense and learn all the plays. As a running back, I just have to use my natural running ability. That's a lot easier."

Teams now paid Jerome Bettis the ultimate compliment: To beat the Rams, you first have to stop him. "Teams we play from here on out are not going to say they have to stop T. J. Rubley or Henry Ellard or Flipper Anderson," said Rams offensive coordinator Ernie Zampese. "They're going to have to stop Jerome Bettis and the running game."

The Rams did not try to hide their preference for giving the ball to Bettis. "I think we'll go out and try to dominate the line of scrimmage and the offensive line and Jerome will take us where we want to go," said Coach Zampese.

The Rams' record fell to 4-10 in a 15-3 loss to the Cincinnati Bengals. But Jerome Bettis ran for 124 yards—his fourth consecutive game over the 100-yard mark—and took sole position of the NFL rushing lead with two games to play. He could have had even more yards. But he did not play in the fourth quarter because the Rams were down 12-3, and needed to pass the football. Bettis, however, was more concerned with the loss to the Bengals than with his personal statistics. "You have to put everything in perspective," he said after the game. "If I'm getting it done, but I'm not helping the team win, what good is it? What we've got to do is find a way to put some points on the board."

No NFL rookie had won the rushing title since the Rams' Eric Dickerson did it in 1983. Jerome Bettis realized it would be difficult for a rookie to win the title over the Dallas Cowboys' Emmitt Smith, the Detroit Lions' Barry Sanders, or the Buffalo Bills' Thurman Thomas. "I still think I'm the underdog in this race," said Bettis. "It just feels great to be in the same company with these guys."

Coach Knox and the rest of the Rams hoped Bettis would win the rushing title and the rookie of the year award. "He's done an outstanding job," said Coach Knox. "One, because of the changes in the offensive line we've had, and two, with teams giving us a lot of different fronts, they have also given us a variety of alignments trying to confuse our new people. His performance is more remarkable because of that."

In the next to last game of the season, the Cleveland Browns blew out the Rams, 42-14. Jerome Bettis carried the ball just 16 times for 56 yards. He was thirty-five yards behind Emmitt Smith for the NFL rushing title. The Browns' stingy defense did not surprise Bettis. "[The Browns] came into the game knowing they weren't going to be beaten by the run," he said.

In the final game of the season, Jerome Bettis did everything in his power to help the Rams beat the Chicago Bears. He also hoped he would help himself to win the rushing title. Going into the game, however, Bettis played down his chances of winning the title. "I don't think I have a great chance of doing it because the Bears are tough and have the fifth-ranked defense," he said. "But that doesn't mean I won't be trying to make it happen."

Bettis had 146 yards and one touchdown on 39 carries. The Rams defeated the Bears, 20-6. Bettis also caught the football 5 times for 71 yards. His 39 rushes broke Eric Dickerson's Ram record of 38 carries in a single game. Coach Knox called a timeout with 5 seconds remaining in the game to give Bettis an opportunity to break the record. "I didn't have any problem with [calling a timeout]," Coach Knox says. "I felt he deserved the record the way he had run."

Unfortunately, Jerome Bettis did not win the NFL rushing

In a game against Chicago, Bettis broke a Rams' record by running the ball thirty-nine times.

title. Emmitt Smith rushed for 168 yards against the New York Giants. This gave him 1,486 yards and his third consecutive rushing title. Bettis complimented Emmitt Smith. "Big players play big games and Emmitt showed that by having a big game and putting a lot of pressure on me."

Bettis's 1,429 yards in 1993, however, was the seventh-best single-season total for a rookie in NFL history. It was the fourth-best mark in Rams history and the second-highest total for a Rams rookie. Jerome Bettis was selected to play in the Pro Bowl. He also shared the NFL rookie of the year award with Rick Mirer. *The Sporting News* named Bettis its offensive rookie of the year.

Jerome Bettis proved during his rookie year that he could tip-toe through the line of scrimmage as well as pound out the yards like a typical power back. How did he make the transition from fullback in college to tailback in the NFL so easily? "I changed my style a bit. At Notre Dame, I was concerned with making productive yards in traffic. In the NFL, I'm picking my spots a little more and using my footwork to break free. It was just a natural thing that happened as I got comfortable in the offense."

To end his fairy-tale rookie season, Jerome Bettis scored a touchdown in the Pro Bowl to help the NFC to a 17-3 victory over the American Football Conference (AFC).

After the season, Bettis had a chance to look back on his rookie achievements. "After the season was over, it started to sink in. I had a lot of personal goals, but I never put them before the team. My biggest goal was to win games."

Chapter 5

Jerome Bettis had high expectations for the 1994 season. He playfully predicted that he would become the third running back in NFL history to rush for more than 2,000 yards in a season. In the last six games of 1993, Bettis averaged 131 yards rushing per game. To rush for 2,000 yards, he would have to average only 125. "My goal is 2,000 yards this year, and if Emmitt [Smith] is setting his goal anything short of that, then he's going to be a little short when it comes time for someone to win the rushing title," Bettis said before the 1994 season.

Jerome Bettis was now one of the top tailbacks in the league. But the Rams were still in a rebuilding mode. No one expected them to do much better than their 5-11 record of 1993. Bettis was one of only a few players that the Rams could count on to perform well week after week. This was good and bad for Bettis. He could expect to carry the ball a lot. If the Rams became too predictable on offense, however, defenses would have an easy time stopping Jerome Bettis and the Rams' running game.

Facing the Cardinals in the first game of the 1994 season was a big test for Bettis and the Rams. Cardinals head coach Buddy Ryan was a defensive specialist who took pride in stopping the run. Bettis carried the ball 21 times for just 52 yards and one touchdown as the Rams nipped the Cardinals, 14-12. "Coming in, I was not expecting a super-big day," Bettis said after the game. "I knew they had a great defense."

In the Rams' next game, Bettis ran for 102 yards on 24 carries in a losing effort against the Atlanta Falcons. The Battering Ram continued to run well against the eventual Super Bowl XXIX champion San Francisco 49ers. In the first half Bettis gained 70 yards on 17 carries and helped the Rams stay close to San Francisco. The 49ers, however, built a 21-point lead in the second half. Bettis carried the ball only four more times. Bettis finished the game with 104 yards and one touchdown.

Behind Bettis's running, the Rams evened their record at 2-2 with a 16-0 shutout of the Kansas City Chiefs. With solid ball control offense, the Rams held the ball for 34 minutes compared to 26 for the Chiefs. Bettis ran the football 35 times for 132 yards.

In the second half, the Rams showed how much they relied on Jerome Bettis. With 8:47 remaining in the third quarter, the Rams led 13-0. For the rest of the game, they ran twenty-two plays. Seventeen of the plays were rushes by Jerome Bettis and two of them were receptions by him. "When we had to have it, he got the job done," Coach Knox said of Bettis.

Bettis's performance did not escape the notice of Rams guard Tom Newberry. "You're down on the ground with your guy, and you look up and he's still going," said Newberry. "He's got three guys hanging on him, and he's struggling to get a few more yards."

Bettis has success against even the best teams. In a 1994 game against the 49ers, Bettis was able to gain 104 yards.

The Rams fell to 2-3 in an ugly 8-5 loss to the Atlanta Falcons. But there seemed to be no stopping Jerome Bettis. He carried the ball 29 times for 117 yards—his fourth consecutive game of over 100 yards rushing.

Through the first five games of the 1994 season, Jerome Bettis accounted for 40 percent of the Rams' total yards on offense. He faced eight-man fronts aimed at stopping him. But Jerome Bettis still had 507 yards rushing. Only Detroit's Barry Sanders and Pittsburgh's Barry Foster had more yards rushing than that. Bettis's development as a running back impressed Coach Knox. "He's made great strides," said Coach Knox. "He's been catching the ball out of the backfield. He's just a very powerful running back."

Jerome Bettis refused to take all the credit for his success. "It hasn't just been me in there running over eight guys. My offensive line has been doing a great job finding me holes and getting me creases. Fortunately, I've been able to get through them in enough time to get up the field."

Bettis carried the ball twenty-five to thirty times a game. Defenses were geared to stop him. His body began to feel the pain of many tackles. Jerome Bettis hoped that the Rams' passing attack would improve so that the team would not have to rely on him so much. With a more balanced offense, he could stay fresh for the whole season. Unfortunately, the Rams never found balance on offense, and Bettis began to take even more of a pounding.

Bettis rushed for 507 yards in the Rams' first five games of the 1994 season. He rushed for only 518 yards in the final eleven games. He came close to rushing for over 100 yards in only two of those games. Not surprisingly, the Rams won both of those games. In a 17-10 victory over the New York Giants, Bettis ran for 88 yards on 30 carries. He rushed for 91

In 1994, the game plan of opposing defenses was to stop Jerome Bettis.
However, Bettis still managed to be effective.

yards and a touchdown in the Rams' 27-21 win over the Denver Broncos.

The victory over the Broncos put the Rams' record at 4-5. If the Rams could play a little better in the second half of the season, they had a chance to make the playoffs. However, the unthinkable happened. The Rams lost all of their last seven games. One of those losses came against the Raiders (then playing in Los Angeles). Raiders defensive tackle Chester McGlockton expressed what every team playing the Rams knew. "We had to stop the run. Jerome Bettis is a heck of a back. We knew if we could stop him, then we could just come off and rush the passer."

There was an off-field distraction to add to the Rams' on-field problems. Dwindling fan support led to speculation that the Rams would leave Los Angeles and move to St. Louis, Missouri, after the 1994 season.

True, the Rams suffered through a seven-game losing streak and there was controversy surrounding their proposed move. Still, Jerome Bettis finished the season with 1,025 yards rushing. This was the fifth-highest total in the NFC. He was also named to the Pro Bowl for the second straight year. He was the first Ram since Eric Dickerson to make the Pro Bowl in his first two NFL seasons. Jerome Bettis was also the first Ram to rush for 1,000 yards in consecutive seasons since Greg Bell did it in 1988 and 1989.

No one on the Rams suffered more than Jerome Bettis during the losing streak. Four starting offensive linemen were injured and Bettis took quite a beating. The Rams finished the season with a 4-12 record. Bettis blamed poor teamwork for the Rams horrible 1994 season. "No one committed. People were more committed to doing other things and being in tune with themselves rather than in being in tune with the team."

The Rams made sweeping changes before the 1995

Jerome Bettis became the first Ram since Eric Dickerson to be selected to the Pro-Bowl team in each of his first two seasons.

season. The team moved to St. Louis and brought in Rich Brooks as head coach. Coach Brooks planned to ease the burden on Jerome Bettis. He would use two tight ends on running plays and use Bettis as a receiver more often. The Rams signed fullback Leonard Russell and offensive guard Dwayne White to open holes for Bettis. "I think that can only excite Bettis," said Coach Brooks.

Jerome Bettis hoped to ease the wear and tear on his body in 1995. But, winning football games was his primary concern. "Another bad year like last year could frustrate me to no end," Bettis said before the 1995 season. "The only commitment that I want from the Rams is a commitment to win."

Chapter 6

The Rams began the 1995 season with an optimism that had been missing during the last few years. The move to St. Louis energized the team. Tickets for all home games were sold out. Team merchandise was scarce. Nonetheless, experts did not expect much of an improvement from the Rams' 4-12 record in 1994.

Jerome Bettis entered the season with a chance to reach some milestones for a player in only his third professional year. He had a chance to join Eric Dickerson as the only two players in Rams history to rush for 1,000 yards in their first three seasons. Bettis also needed just 398 yards to move into the Rams' top ten all-time rushing list.

The Rams' first game of the 1995 season seemed like a replay of the final seven games of 1994. Bettis carried the ball 7 times for a total of only 4 yards. This was the lowest single-game total of his career. Luckily, the Rams managed to defeat the Green Bay Packers, 17-14. Some observers, however, began to wonder whether Jerome Bettis was losing his speed or aggressiveness.

Bettis quieted all the doubters in the Rams' home opener against the New Orleans Saints. The Battering Ram ran for 83 yards on 12 carries. He helped the Rams win, 17-13. After the game, Jerome's teammates came to his defense. "He got a bum rap," said offensive guard Dwayne White. "I don't think it was him struggling, it was just a matter of all of us coming together as one."

As Jerome Bettis was regaining his running form, the Rams started off at 2-0. Their next game was against the Carolina Panthers. This was an expansion team playing in its first season in the NFL. The Rams had an excellent chance to go to 3-0.

As expected, the Rams rolled to a 31-10 victory over the Panthers. Jerome Bettis ran the ball 19 times for 67 yards. He had a 2-yard touchdown run in the second quarter that put the Rams ahead for good. The Rams' 3-0 start elated the team and the fans of St. Louis.

Bettis now had a couple of good games under his belt. He expected himself and the team to get even better as the season progressed. "It's all predicated on how guys up front do," he said. "They're good but still . . . having some mental breakdowns over who they should block, but there are no problems with the intensity."

The Rams and Jerome Bettis anticipated a tough game against the Chicago Bears, their next opponent. The Rams trailed 21-17 at halftime but looked to Bettis in the second half. The Rams scored two touchdowns in the third quarter. Jerome Bettis carried the ball 7 times for 40 yards in that quarter. This was simply too much for the Bears. "We didn't know Bettis would do as good a job as he did," said Bears defensive back Donnell Woolford. "He kept us off balance."

For the game, Jerome finished with 74 yards on 22 carries. Jerome took a moment to reassure those who thought

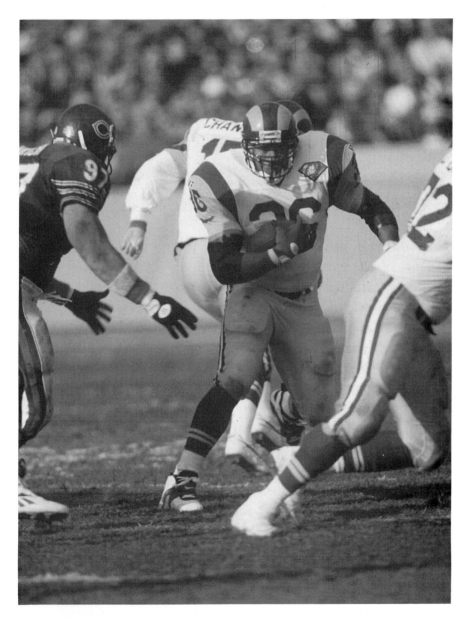

Bettis is one of the best running backs in the NFL. A Pro Football Hall of Fame committee named him to the NFL's All-Decade Team of the 1990s.

he might have lost a step. "I don't think I was ever gone," he said. "It's just that offensively we're still learning schemes and coming together."

The Rams were now 4-0. They had won a *total* of four games in 1994. The victory marked the first time the Rams won four games in a row since 1989. How had the Rams turned around their fortunes so quickly?

The Rams were less predictable on offense than in 1994. "Jack Reilly, our [new] offensive coordinator, has come in and done a whole lot to take away that predictability that was on the offense," explained Bettis. The offensive line was also playing better, which enabled Jerome Bettis to play well. "Each game [the offensive line has] gotten better and better and I think my productivity has gotten better each game right along with them," Bettis said.

Turnovers (taking the ball away from the other team by an interception or fumble recovery) were the other reason that the Rams were 4-0. The Rams had forced 14 turnovers, but had not turned the ball over themselves in their first four games. This tied an NFL record for consecutive games without committing a turnover.

The Rams finally lost their first game of the season to the Indianapolis Colts, 21-18. The Colts came into the game trying to stop the run. Their defensive line dominated the Rams' offensive line. "I don't think we overlooked them," said Bettis, who carried the ball for only 31 yards. "They just outplayed us. They did a great job keeping the pressure on and taking the running game away from us." The Rams also committed their first three turnovers of the season.

Jerome Bettis and the Rams had to shake off the loss to the Colts in a hurry. Their next opponent was the 4-1 Atlanta Falcons. Behind the legs of Jerome Bettis and the hands of wide receiver Isaac Bruce, the Rams won, 21-19. Bruce

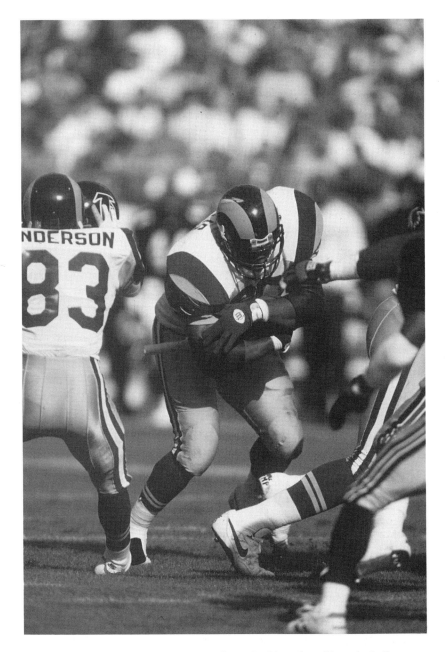

In a 1995 game against Atlanta, Bettis ran for 88 yards and kept the ball out of the hands of the Falcon offense. St. Louis won the game, 21-19, to start the season at 5-1.

provided the big plays on offense. He caught 10 passes for 191 yards and 2 touchdowns. Jerome Bettis, however, was instrumental in keeping the ball away from the Falcons quick-strike "red gun" offense. He ran the ball 19 times for 88 yards to give the Rams a decisive time-of-possession advantage.

The Rams started the season with a 5-1 record. But they lost their next three games. They fell behind early to the Super Bowl champion San Francisco 49ers and had to abandon the running game. Jerome Bettis carried the ball only 11 times for 34 yards in the 44-10 loss. He aggravated a foot injury and sat out most of the game in the Rams' 20-9 loss to the Philadelphia Eagles. In that game he rushed the ball 10 times for only 27 yards. However, Bettis moved into tenth place on the Rams' all-time rushing list.

At the halfway point of the season, Bettis had gained only 408 yards on 119 carries. "It seems like we're a person away from breaking it," said Bettis. "As soon as I make a break and start to get in the open, someone comes from behind. I don't think we've gotten to the point where we're clicking on all cylinders."

Another reason for Bettis's relatively low rushing output was the offensive philosophy of Head Coach Rich Brooks. Coach Brooks passed the ball more than Coach Knox, Bettis's coach during his first two years in the NFL. In 1994 Bettis averaged 20 rushing attempts per game. The Rams as a team averaged 32 pass attempts per game. Under Coach Brooks, however, Jerome Bettis averaged just 12 carries. The Rams averaged 40 passes.

The Rams started the second half of the season against the 2-6 New Orleans Saints. Bettis's sprained left foot forced him to miss the first game of his three-year career. Without Jerome Bettis in the lineup the Rams struggled on offense. They lost the game, 19-10.

Despite their three-game losing streak, the Rams were still in the hunt for a playoff spot. Bettis came back strong in the Rams' next game against the Carolina Panthers. He carried the ball 26 times for 91 yards and a touchdown. Bettis's running kept the ball out of the hands of the Panthers' offense. St. Louis won easily, 28-17.

Jerome Bettis finally had a long run in the Rams' eleventh game of the season. He took a handoff from quarterback Chris Miller. He darted through a hole on the left side of the line of scrimmage. He broke a few tackles and raced up the sideline for a 41-yard gain. Unfortunately, the Rams trailed the Atlanta Falcons for most of the game. Bettis carried the ball a total of 9 times for only 61 yards. The Rams lost the game, 31-6.

Things did not get any easier for Jerome Bettis and the Rams during their second meeting of the season with the San Francisco 49ers. At halftime the Rams were down 28-7. Not surprisingly they abandoned the running game in the second half. Jerome Bettis finished the day with only 6 rushing attempts for 20 yards. The 49ers trounced the Rams, 41-13.

In the Rams' next game Jerome Bettis carried the ball only 8 times for 20 yards. But the Rams managed to squeak by the New York Jets, 23-20. The Rams improved their record to 7-6. Unfortunately, that was the Rams' last win of the season. In the Rams' final three games, Jerome Bettis carried the ball just 15 times for only 45 yards. The Rams were outscored by their opponents, 121-72.

Jerome Bettis finished the season with a team-high 637 yards rushing. He became only the fourth player in Rams history to lead the team in rushing for three consecutive seasons. In just his third NFL season, Jerome's 3,091 career yards placed him ninth on the Rams' all-time rushing list.

After the season, the Rams traded defensive end Sean

After only three seasons with the Rams, Bettis was the ninth-leading
rusher in team history.

Gilbert to the Washington Redskins. In return they received sixth overall pick in the 1996 NFL draft. Experts speculated that if the Rams could draft a decent running back with that pick, they would trade Jerome Bettis for even more draft picks. This would help them to build their team. This is exactly what happened in April 1996. Jerome Bettis was traded to the Pittsburgh Steelers, the defending AFC (American Football Conference) champions. In exchange the Rams received a second-round and fourth-round draft pick.

Both the Steelers and Jerome Bettis were happy about the deal. The Steelers traditionally prefer to run the football. With their young quarterbacks Kordell Stewart and Jim Miller, they probably will be inclined to run the football even more in 1996. "It makes us feel good to be able to get a player the caliber of Jerome Bettis to come into this style of offense, which we feel suits his abilities," said Tom Donahoe, Pittsburgh's director of football operations. The Steelers also helped their running game by drafting an offensive lineman and a blocking back.

Career Statistics

YEAR	TEAM	RUSHING				PASS RECEIVING			
		Carries	Yards	Avg.	TDs	Rec.	Yards	Avg.	TDs
1993	L.A. Rams	294	1,429	4.9	7	26	244	9.4	0
1994	L.A. Rams	319	1,025	3.2	3	31	293	9.5	1
1995	St. Louis Rams	183	637	3.5	3	18	106	5.9	0
TOTAL		796	3,091	3.9	13	75	643	8.6	1

AVG-Average
TDs-Touchdowns
REC-Receptions

Where to Write Jerome Bettis

Mr. Jerome Bettis
c/o Pittsburgh Steelers
300 Stadium Circle
Pittsburgh, PA 15212-5721

Index

A

AFC, 41, 59
All-America team, 25, 27, 31
Anderson, Flipper, 38
Anthony, Earl, 16
Arizona Cardinals, 44
Atlanta Falcons, 35, 44, 46, 54, 56, 57

B

Bailey, Carlton, 13
Beck, Tom, 24
Bell, Greg, 48
Bettis, Gladys, 15, 16, 18
Bettis, Johnnie, 16
Bettis, Kimberly, 16
Boykin, Deral, 8
Brooks, Rich, 48, 50, 56
Bruce, Isaac, 54, 56
Buffalo Bills, 39

C

Carolina Panthers, 52, 57
Carter, Pat, 10
Chicago Bears, 39, 52
Cincinnati Bengals, 38
Cleveland Browns, 39
Culver, Rodney, 23

D

Dallas Cowboys, 7, 38, 39
David MacKenzie High School, 18
Denver Broncos, 46, 48
Detroit, 13, 15, 16
Detroit Lions, 37, 39, 46
Detroit Public School League, 19
Dickerson, Eric, 12, 38, 39, 48, 51
Donahoe, Tom, 59

E

Ellard, Henry, 38
Everett, Jim, 35,37

F

Florida, University of, 27
Foster, Barry, 46

G

Gary, Cleveland, 33, 35
Gator Bowl, 31
Gilbert, Sean, 57, 59
Goeas, Leo, 8
Green Bay Packers, 33, 51

H

Heisman Trophy, 27, 28, 30, 31, 38
Henry Ford High School, 18
Holtz, Lou, 19, 21, 23, 28
Holtz, Skip, 19, 21
Houston Oilers, 35

I

Indiana University, 24
Indianapolis Colts, 54

J

Jackson, Bo, 10
Johnson, Anthony, 24

K

Kansas City Chiefs, 44
Knox, Chuck, 12, 13, 33, 35, 39, 44, 46, 56

L

Lester, Tim, 8
Los Angeles Raiders, 48
Los Angeles Rams, 7, 8, 10, 12, 33, 35, 37, 38, 39, 43, 44, 46, 48

M

McGlockton, Chester, 48
Michigan State University, 24, 28
Michigan, University of, 19, 28
Miller, Chris, 57

Miller, Jim, 59
Miller-Digby Memorial Award, 27
Mills, Sam, 8, 12
Mirer, Rick, 24, 27, 30, 37, 38, 41

N

Navy (United States Naval Academy), 24
New Orleans Saints, 7, 8, 10, 12, 35, 37, 52, 56
New York Giants, 13, 35, 41, 46
New York Jets, 57
Newberry, Tom, 10, 44
NFC, 12, 41, 48
NFL, 7, 10, 12, 18, 19, 31, 37, 38, 41, 48, 52, 54, 56, 57
NFL draft, 31, 33, 59
Northwestern University, 28
Notre Dame, University of, 12, 19, 21, 23, 24, 25, 27, 28, 30, 31, 38, 41

P

Pennsylvania State University, 30
Phoenix Cardinals, 37
Philadelphia Eagles, 56
Pittsburgh Steelers, 35, 46, 59
Pittsburgh, University of, 24, 30
Pro Bowl, 15, 41, 48
Purdue University, 28

R

"Red-gun" offense, 56
Reilly, Jack, 54
rookie of the year award, 37, 38, 39, 41
Rubley, T.J., 8, 10, 35, 37, 38
Russell, Leonard, 50
Ryan, Buddy, 44

S

San Francisco 49ers, 25, 28, 37, 44, 56, 57
Sanders, Barry, 39, 46
Seattle Seahawks, 37
Slater, Jackie, 10
Smith, Emmitt, 7, 39, 41, 43
Smith, Irv, 30
Smith, Larry, 25
St. Louis Rams, 48, 50, 51, 52, 54, 56, 57
Stanford University, 24, 28, 30
Stewart, Kordell, 59
Sugar Bowl, 27
Super Bowl, 25, 28, 44, 56

T

Tennessee, University of, 25
Texas A&M University, 31
Thomas, Thurman, 39
turnovers, 54

U

USC (University of Southern California), 25, 30

W

Walsh, Bill, 25, 28
Washington Redskins, 37, 59
White, Dwayne, 50, 52
Williams, James, 7
Wilson, Tom, 10
Woodford, Donnell, 52

Z

Zampese, Ernie, 36